We Are Beautiful

Kingdom Publishing, LLC
Odenton, MD 21113

Printed in the United States of America

copyright ©2023 by Kimberly Curtis

ISBN: 978-1-947741-85-0

All rights reserved. No part of this book may be reproduced or transmitted in any form or by any means
without written permission of the author.

Cover design and book illustration by
Antonio M. Palmer

This book was inspired by my beautiful twin daughters, Ravyn and Rylei. I dedicate this book to my parents and all the parents who inspire their children to find the beauty in themselves and others.

The world is full of beauty.
All you have to do is open your eyes
and look around.
Beauty is in everything you see.
Beauty is in everything you touch.
It's in the wind that blows
and the flowers that grow.
Welcome to our world of beauty!

Beauty is in the town,
Beauty is all around,

Beauty is in our flare,
Beauty is in our hair,

Beauty is in our dance,
Beauty is in our stance,

Beauty is in the way we care,
Beauty is in our prayer,

**Beauty is style,
Beauty is in our smile,**

Beauty is in our kindness,
Beauty is in our brightness,

Beauty is in our mind,
Beauty is one of a kind,

Beauty is in our walk,
Beauty is in our talk,

**Beauty is in our attitude,
Beauty is in our gratitude,**

Beauty comes from within and
Beauty radiates from our skin,

Beauty is our joy inside,
Beauty is something we won't hide!

No matter what your beautiful is,
make sure you find it!
Beauty is just being YOU!
We are beautiful!

www.ingramcontent.com/pod-product-compliance
Lightning Source LLC
Chambersburg PA
CBHW050753110526
44592CB00002B/47